3 8011 00195 1394

MW00979128

3

A Smart Kid's
Guide to
Personal Finance

How to Save and Invest

Ryan Randolph

PowerKiDS
press.

New York

Published in 2014 by The Rosen Publishing Group, Inc.
29 East 21st Street, New York, NY 10010

First Edition

Editor: Jennifer Way
Book Design: Greg Tucker

Photo Credits: Cover © iStockphoto.com/Bryan Creely; p. 5 Gallo Images/Getty Images; p. 6 Ryan McVay/Photodisc/Thinkstock; p. 7 Edyta Pawlowska/Shutterstock.com; p. 8 Robert Kneschke/Shutterstock.com; p. 9 Yuri Arcurs/Shutterstock.com; p. 10 Gina Smith/Shutterstock.com; p. 11 (top) Sean Murphy/Lifesize/Thinkstock.com; p. 11 (bottom) Andy Dean Photography/Shutterstock.com; p. 12 Orhan Cam/Shutterstock.com; p. 13 JGI/Jamie Grill/Blend Images/Getty Images; p. 14 Joff Lee/Photolibrary/Getty Images; p. 15 (top) Songquan Deng/Shutterstock.com; p. 15 (bottom) Jeffrey Coolidge/The Image Bank/Getty Images; p. 17 Goodluz/Shutterstock.com; p. 18 AISPIX by Image Source/Shutterstock.com; p. 19 Iva Barmina/Shutterstock.com; p. 21 Adie Bush/Cultura/Getty Images; p. 22 Paul Bradbury/OJO Images/Getty Images.

Library of Congress Cataloging-in-Publication Data

Randolph, Ryan P.
 How to save and invest / by Ryan Randolph. — 1st ed.
    p. cm. — (A smart kid's guide to personal finance)
 Includes index.
 ISBN 978-1-4777-0742-5 (library binding) — ISBN 978-1-4777-0825-5 (pbk.) —
 ISBN 978-1-4777-0826-2 (6-pack)
 1. Investments—Juvenile literature. 2. Saving and investment—Juvenile literature. I. Title.
 HG4521.R282 2014
 332.6—dc23
                          2012043668

Manufactured in the United States of America

CPSIA Compliance Information: Batch #S13PK5: For Further Information contact Rosen Publishing, New York, New York at 1-800-237-9932

Contents

Making Money Work

Savings accounts, **bonds**, and **stocks** are ways to save and **invest** that you may have heard about. Some people call saving and investing "making your money work for you."

Saving is holding on to the money you have. Investing means using the money you have to earn more money. For example, you make an investment when you open a lemonade stand. You invest money that you already have to buy ingredients and paper cups. Your goal is to make more money from selling the lemonade than you put into setting up your stand. If you achieve this goal, the money you invested in the stand helped you make more money!

Earning money can be fun and rewarding. Learning how to save and invest some of that money will make your money grow faster.

Growing Money Through Interest

If you regularly add money to a savings account, the interest you earn will start to add up!

Saving money in your piggy bank earns you no extra money. If you put $100 in there, the amount will stay $100 as long as you keep it there.

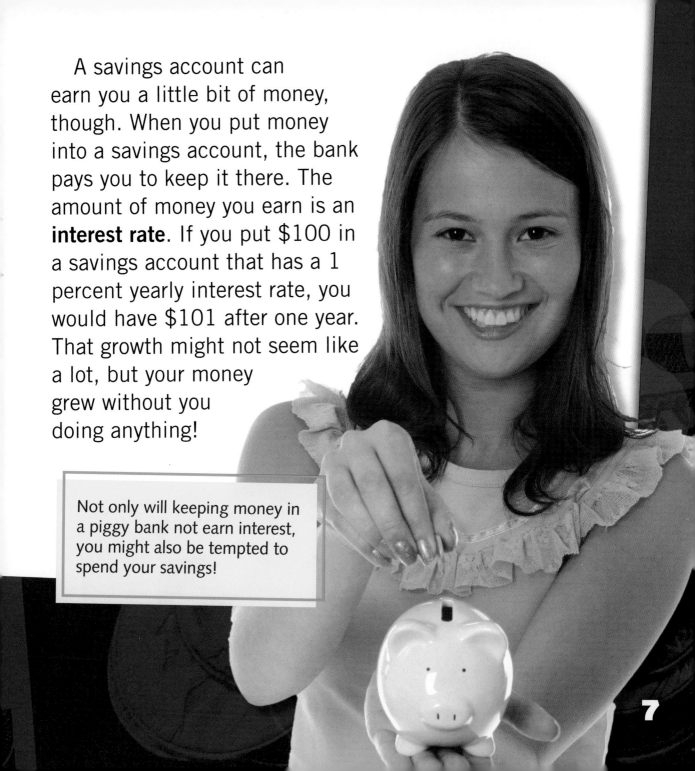

A savings account can earn you a little bit of money, though. When you put money into a savings account, the bank pays you to keep it there. The amount of money you earn is an **interest rate**. If you put $100 in a savings account that has a 1 percent yearly interest rate, you would have $101 after one year. That growth might not seem like a lot, but your money grew without you doing anything!

Not only will keeping money in a piggy bank not earn interest, you might also be tempted to spend your savings!

Why Invest?

Investing can make your money grow, but it can also make you lose money. This is called **risk**. Different investments have different levels of risk. For example, putting money into a savings account is low risk. You earn a steady, small amount of money for keeping your money there. Investing money in stocks is higher risk. The stocks could become worth more money or less money.

Some people get very upset when their investments lose money. They may prefer making lower-risk investments.

Many people meet with a professional called a financial advisor. This person helps people decide what kinds of savings and investment choices are right for them.

Why do people invest and risk losing money, then? For many people, the risk is worth it because they can make more money. They prefer taking a risk and possibly making a lot of money to making a guaranteed but much smaller amount of money.

Saving and Investing for Long-Term Goals

Some parents start saving for their kid's college education when their child is very young. This gives them lots of time to save up the money needed for this expense.

Saving and investing help people achieve long-term goals. These goals are years in the future and require a lot of money. Long-term goals may include buying a house, paying for college, or **retiring**.

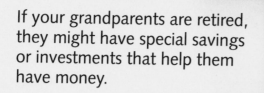

If your grandparents are retired, they might have special savings or investments that help them have money.

People might open a savings account where they put money toward a long-term goal. Later, they will have the money they put in the account and the interest they have earned. People may also open special accounts where the money in them is invested. Later, the money earned from their investments is often much more than the amount they put in. This is why investing can help people reach long-term goals faster than by savings alone.

Long-term goals, such as buying a house, are often met through a combination of savings and investments.

What Are Bonds?

When you invest in a bond, you are lending money to the issuer for a period of time. The issuer could be a company or the government. The issuer promises a time at which it will pay back the amount of the bond with interest. This interest is usually higher than the interest earned by a savings account.

The United States Treasury, shown here, issues government bonds.

For example, if you buy a $100 bond, you lend the issuer $100. If it is a 10-year bond, the issuer will also pay you interest every year for 10 years. If the bond pays 5 percent yearly interest, you will have $150 when the bond **matures** in 10 years.

If you have ever borrowed money from someone and promised to pay it back after a certain amount of time, that is a little bit like how bonds work.

What Are Stocks?

Stocks are a type of investment in which people give companies money in exchange for shares. A share represents a piece of the company. People who own shares of stock in a company are called shareholders or stockholders.

Do you have a favorite soft drink? It is possible that the soda company offers shares for people to invest in.

The center of trading stocks in the United States is on Wall Street in New York City, shown here.

The goal of buying stocks is for the money you invest to grow along with the company. As the company grows and makes more money, the shares of its stock increase in value. Of course, if the company does not do well, its shares can decrease in value. That means that the risk of investing in stocks is that you can lose money. You can also make money, though.

These are stock certificates, which can be issued to investors by companies. People choose stocks based on things such as liking that company's products or believing that the company will do well.

Are There Other Ways to Invest?

Choosing stocks to invest in is hard. People usually own stocks in more than one company at once. This spreads out their risk as their different stocks increase or decrease in value. One way to invest in many stocks is through a **mutual fund**. People put money into the fund, which then invests in different stocks.

There are other ways to invest, such as in **real estate**. An investor might buy a building and rent it out to other people. She might also buy land and build something on it and sell it. In either case, she hopes to earn more money than she invested when she bought the real estate.

A real estate investor might buy land and build something on it. This is called developing.

17

Smart Saving and Investing

When some people invest, they are focused on making money. They want to see their money grow and do not mind the risk involved. Other people are more focused on not losing the money they invest. They will make saving and investment choices that have less risk.

You can follow stock prices and read news about companies in a newspaper.

Another important part of being a smart investor is to research different ways to save and invest. There are many websites and books about this. It is also a good idea to research companies you are interested in investing in. An informed investor is a smart investor!

An important part of becoming a smart investor is knowing how much risk you are comfortable with. This will help you make saving and investment choices that are right for you.

Ways Kids Can Save and Invest

Are you ready to get started saving and investing? There are a few ways kids can practice. First, start saving! Many banks allow kids to open savings accounts. Ask your parents about setting one up.

Is stock market investing more your style? Think about companies that make things you like. Most big companies have stock. For example, if you love video games, you might be interested in the company Electronic Arts. Look up the company's stock price on the Internet and watch how it changes from day to day. Look for news about the company to learn more about it.

If your piggy bank gets full at home, you might want to ask your parents if you could open a savings account.

Smart Saving and Investing Tips

1. Learn more. Ask your parents or librarian to help you find websites and books with information about ways kids can save and invest.

2. There are online games that allow you to pretend to buy real stock. These games allow you to track how your investments would do if you were really investing.

3. Set a goal and stick to it. If you decide to put part of your allowance or earnings in a savings account, do it! Watch the money add up.

4. The key to success in investing is selling something for more than you paid for it. There is a saying, "buy low, sell high," for this kind of investment success.

5. There are fees with some kinds of investments. Smart investors do research to understand the costs that come with investing.

Glossary

bonds (BONDZ) Investments in which people loan money to an issuer for a period of time. The money is then paid back with interest.

interest rate (IN-teh-rest RAYT) The amount of money that the bank pays someone with a savings account.

invest (in-VEST) To put money into something, such as a company, in the hope of getting more money later on.

matures (muh-TOORZ) Is due to be paid back.

mutual fund (MYOO-chuh-wul FUND) An investment company that invests people's money in a group of stocks.

real estate (REEL es-TAYT) The business of selling land and houses.

retiring (rih-TY-ur-ing) Giving up an office or other career.

risk (RISK) The chance that one could suffer harm or loss.

stocks (STOKS) Pieces or shares of a company.

Index

Websites

Due to the changing nature of Internet links, PowerKids Press has developed an online list of websites related to the subject of this book. This site is updated regularly. Please use this link to access the list: www.powerkidslinks.com/skgpf/save/